WHERE YOU LIVE MATTERS: DEVELOPING A VISION FOR YOUR CITY

Q Society Room

A Group Learning Experience

Five Group Gatherings

NORTON HERBST AND GABE LYONS

ZONDERVAN

Q

ZONDERVAN.com/
AUTHORTRACKER
follow your favorite authors

ZONDERVAN

Where You Live Matters Participant's Guide
Copyright © 2010 Q

Requests for information should be addressed to:

Zondervan, *Grand Rapids, Michigan* 49530

ISBN 978-0-310-32450-8

All Scripture quotations, unless otherwise indicated, are taken from the Holy Bible, *Today's New International Version*™. TNIV®. Copyright © 2001, 2005 by Biblica, Inc.™ Used by permission of Zondervan. All rights reserved worldwide.

Any Internet addresses (websites, blogs, etc.) and telephone numbers printed in this book are offered as a resource. They are not intended in any way to be or imply an endorsement by Zondervan, nor does Zondervan vouch for the content of these sites and numbers for the life of this book.

All rights reserved. No part of this publication may be reproduced, stored in a retrieval system, or transmitted in any form or by any means—electronic, mechanical, photocopy, recording, or any other—except for brief quotations in printed reviews, without the prior permission of the publisher.

Published in association with Yates & Yates, www.yates2.com.

Printed in the United States of America

10 11 12 13 14 15 16 /DCI/ 32 31 30 29 28 27 26 25 24 23 22 21 20 19 18 17 16 15 14 13 12 11 10 9 8 7 6 5 4 3 2 1

where you live matters

TABLE OF CONTENTS

Where You Live Matters 1

Welcome to the Society Room..4

Your Place in Culture 6

Roundtable Discussions 8

Group Gathering One: Grace of the City 11

Q Short: Saving Suburbia: From the Garden to the City 29

Group Gathering Two: From the Garden to the City 45

Group Gathering Three: The Future of the Suburbs 63

Group Gathering Four: Grace in and for the City 79

Culture Shaping Project: Learning While Doing 96

Group Gathering Five: Salt and Light 99

WHERE YOU LIVE MATTERS: DEVELOPING A VISION FOR YOUR CITY

Apartment, condo, or house?

Big yard or no yard?

Walk-in closets … finished basement … three-car garage? Or maybe just a loft in the city.

Where you live matters. It's not just about what you can afford, the square footage you need, or the size of the garage. Maybe it goes much deeper than that. Is it possible that God has a bigger vision for our apartments, houses, and neighborhoods than we do? What about the places we shop, the neighbors we encounter, the cities we call home? In this Q Society Room study, your group will explore a *biblical* perspective on where you live.

Over the next several weeks, your group will discuss God's heart for this world he created and how local places—the cities and neighborhoods in which we live—are central to that. You'll be exposed to what the Bible says regarding cities (who knew there was so much in there?). You'll be encouraged to embrace a theology of place. Your group will discuss recent trends regarding urban and suburban development and try to make sense of their connection to our faith. Get ready to think differently about where you live. God has a vision for your city.

WHERE YOU LIVE MATTERS
WELCOME

WELCOME TO THE SOCIETY ROOM

Q Society Room studies are a new, yet historic way to consider issues of faith and culture in the context of a group learning environment. The Society Rooms of the late 1600s and the Clapham Circle of the early 1800s are riveting examples of small gatherings of leaders that would convene, dialogue, learn, and work together to renew their culture. Consider the impact of these early Society Rooms:

> In 1673 Dr. Anthony Horneck, a Church of England minister in London, preached a number of what he called "awakening sermons." As a result several young men began to meet together weekly in order to build up one another in the Christian faith. They gathered in small groups at certain fixed locations and their places of meeting became known as Society Rooms. In these gatherings they read the Bible, studied religious books and prayed; they also went out among the poor to relieve want at their own expense and to show kindness to all. By 1730 nearly one hundred of these Societies existed in London, and others—perhaps another hundred—were to be found in cities and towns throughout England. The Societies movement became, in many senses, the cradle of the Revival ..." (Arnold Dallimore, *George Whitefield*, Vol. 1, Crossway, 1990, pp. 28–29)

Following this historical example, this group study is designed to renew your minds as leaders so that you can make a difference in society. Society Room communities like yours are characterized by a commitment to put learning into action. And no doubt, over the course of the next few weeks, your innermost beliefs and preconceived ideas about life, faith, the world, and your cultural responsibility will be challenged. But that's the point.

Here's how it works. Your group will gather five times to discuss important topics related to the overall theme of this study. Sometimes you'll be given something to do or read before your group gathers. It's important for you to take these "assignments" seriously. They won't demand much time, but they will require intentionality. Doing these things ahead of time will cultivate a richer and more stimulating group experience as you begin to practice what you are learning.

For each group gathering, set aside about one hour and fifteen minutes for the discussion in a place with minimal distractions. Your group may want to share a meal together first, but be sure to allow enough time for unhurried dialogue to take place. Sometimes you'll watch a short video. But conversation and dialogue will always be the priority. The leader of the group will not teach or lecture, but instead will ask questions, facilitate conversation, and seek input from everyone. Be prepared to ask good questions and share your own thoughts. Sometimes you'll even debate an issue by taking sides and thinking through all the complexities. The goal of each gathering is for your group to be stimulated by a particular idea and learn together as you discuss its impact on your faith, your lives, and culture in general. Your group may not arrive at a consensus regarding any given topic. That's okay. Be respectful of others, even when you disagree with them. We can learn something from everyone.

Before your fifth gathering, you will undertake a group project together. You may be tempted to skip this. Don't! Your group project might be the most important part of your experience. Genuine learning as a community takes place when you engage the ideas you are discussing and do something together as a group.

In the end, be committed to this group and the learning process that is about to ensue. Your willingness to prepare for group gatherings, keep an open mind, and demonstrate eagerness to learn together will pave the way for a great experience.

YOUR PLACE IN CULTURE

INTRODUCTIONS

At the beginning of your first gathering, spend about fifteen minutes introducing yourselves to one another and discussing your channel of cultural influence.

There are several different social institutions that touch every person in a given society. These areas of influence contain most of the industries and organizations that consistently shape our culture. They touch every aspect of our lives, and most of us find our vocational roles in one or more of these areas. They are the seven channels of cultural influence.

As you begin your Society Room experience, you'll notice that most, if not all, of these channels are represented in your group. Start your first gathering by sharing which particular channel of influence you participate in. Give the rest of the group a sense of how your channel contributes to shaping society in general. Then, throughout the rest of the group experience, reflect on how your learning will affect the channel to which you've been called.

7 Channels of Cultural Influence

01
m
media

where you live matters   7

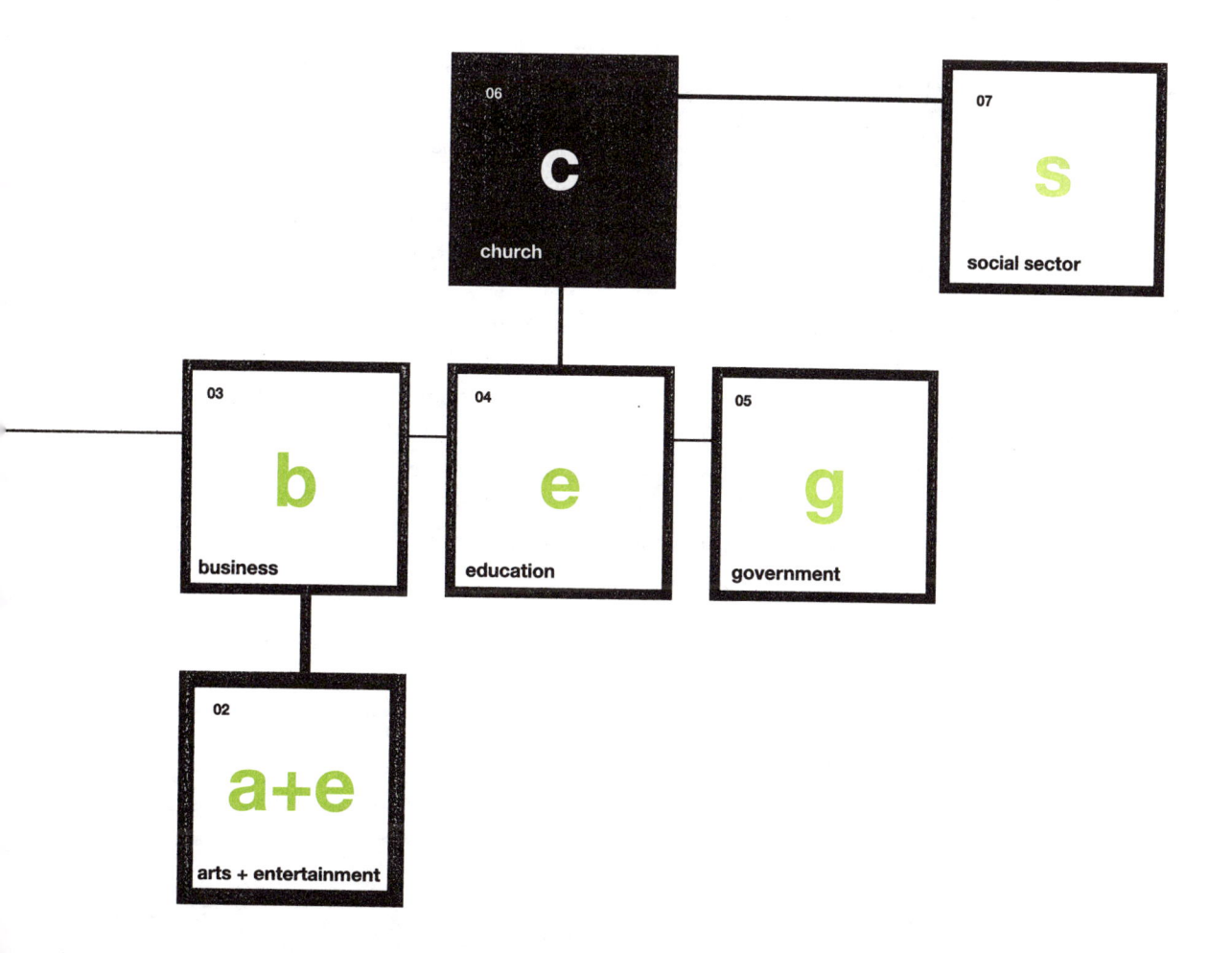

06	07
C church	**s** social sector

03	04	05
b business	**e** education	**g** government

02
a+e arts + entertainment

ROUNDTABLE DISCUSSIONS

As part of this Q Society Room, we convened leaders from various channels of culture to discuss these important topics. Throughout the study, you will be introduced to their thoughts and ideas in hopes of stirring your conversation and dialogue.

Gabe Lyons
Q Founder & Author
Gabe Lyons is the author of *The Next Christians: The Good News About the End of Christian America* and the creator of Q — a learning community that educates Christians on their responsibility and opportunities to renew culture. Lyons coauthored *UnChristian*, a bestselling book that reveals exclusive research on pop culture's negative perception of Christians. Gabe, his wife Rebekah, and their three children reside in Atlanta, Georgia.

Jon Tyson
Pastor, New York City
Jon is a church planter and lead pastor of Trinity Grace Church, located in New York City. He is also on the board of directors of the Origins Movement, a new church planting movement committed to multiplying missional church communities in the major urban centers of the world.

Allie Tsavdarides
Marketing Consultant
Allie is an environmental pupil of unique environments and human behavior. She's lived, traveled, and studied overseas and has learned firsthand how urban community serves as an essential conduit of cultural, artistic, spiritual, and intellectual exploration. Allie is in the business of branding and creative development, but also spends her nights skating with a local roller derby league in Atlanta, Georgia.

Andy Crouch
Author & Journalist
Andy is the author of *Culture Making: Recovering Our Creative Calling* and a senior editor at Christianity Today International. He has served as executive producer of the documentary films *Where Faith and Culture Meet* and *Round Trip* and was editorial director of the Christian Vision Project. He is currently a member of the editorial board of *Books & Culture* and a senior fellow of the International Justice Mission's IJM Institute.

Sean Womack
Branding & Strategy Consultant
Sean's work assignments have included (in no particular chronological order): mowing, warehouse work, bank teller, editorial cartoonist, pasta chef, house cleaning, greeting cards, publishing, entertainment marketing, advertising creative director, marketing VP and brand consultant. Sean is currently founder of TBD, an agency that exists to help people, brands, and organizations determine who they are, where they are going, and how to get there.

This city is what it is because our citizens are what they are.

PLATO

Let the redeemed of the Lord tell their story—
    those he redeemed from the hand of the foe,
those he gathered from the lands,
    from east and west, from north and south.
Some wandered in desert wastelands,
    finding no way to a city where they could settle.
They were hungry and thirsty,
    and their lives ebbed away.
Then they cried out to the Lord in their trouble,
    and he delivered them from their distress.
He led them by a straight way
    to a city where they could settle.

PSALM 107:2–7

GROUP GATHERING ONE
GRACE OF THE CITY

group gathering one

GROWING UP

DISCUSS

Take a few minutes and share with the rest of the group about where you grew up and how it shaped you.

Where we have lived throughout our lives has had a huge impact in shaping who we are. And perhaps most influential are the places we lived during childhood and adolescence. From the general location—small town, big city, suburb, or rural area—to the actual dwelling place—apartment, condo, house or farm—where we grew up is fundamental to our identities.

DISCUSSION STARTERS

Where did you grow up? *Columbia, farm*

Did your family move around or did you stay in one or two places most of your childhood? *stayed*

What kind of relationships did you have with your neighbors or the other people living closest to you? *some close, some not*

How do you now make decisions about where to live, the type of place to rent or own, and how you interact with your neighbors?
safety, handicap accessible

where you live matters   13

HOW MANY PLACES HAVE YOU LIVED?

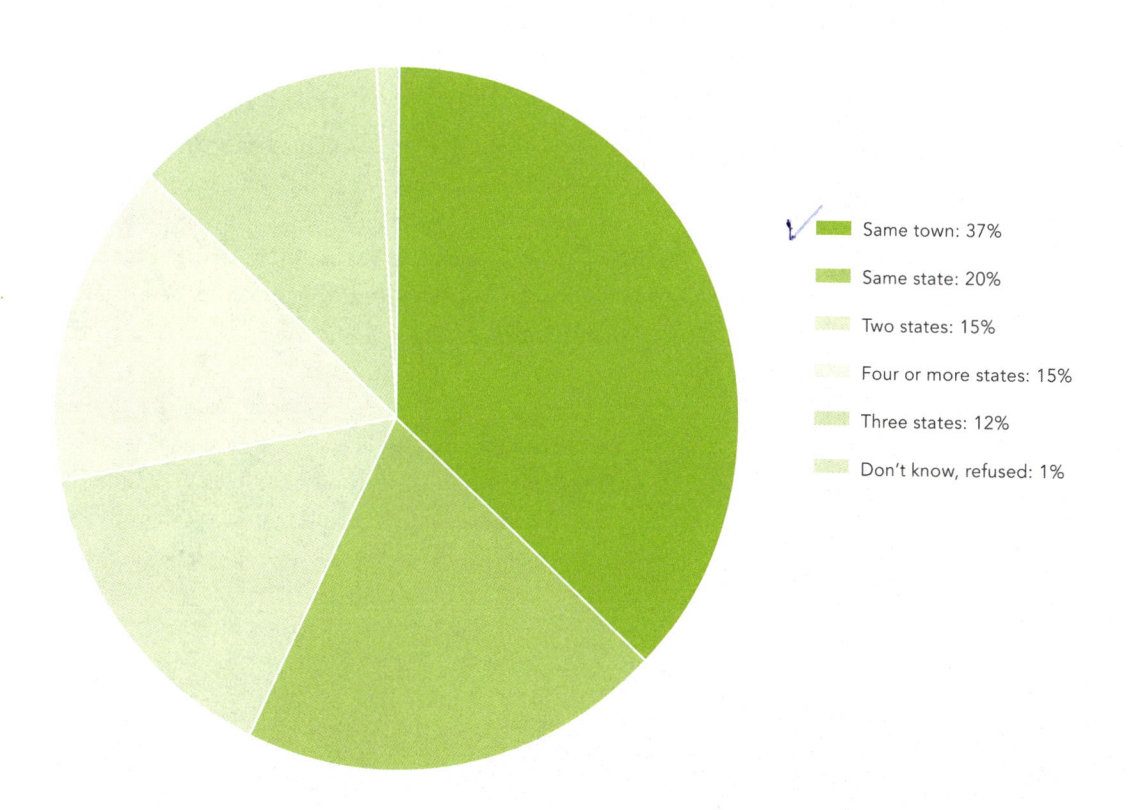

- Same town: 37%
- Same state: 20%
- Two states: 15%
- Four or more states: 15%
- Three states: 12%
- Don't know, refused: 1%

Source: Pew Research Center Social & Demographic Trends Study: "Who Moves? Who Stays Put? Where's Home?" by D'Vera Cohn and Rich Morin, Pew Research Center December 17, 2008 at http://pewsocialtrends.org/pubs/721/movers-and-stayers.

group gathering one

GRACE OF THE CITY

WATCH

View Q Talk: Grace of the City by Timothy Keller.

Record your thoughts on the talk on page 17.

Dr. Timothy J. Keller is senior pastor of Redeemer Presbyterian Church in New York City and author of the *New York Times* bestseller *The Reason For God*. He has lived in Manhattan for over twenty years and is passionate about encouraging Christians and pastors to move to urban areas to be a part of what God is doing there.

At Q New York, Timothy Keller challenged Christian leaders to reconsider where they live in light of God's heart for cities. In this first part of his talk, he contends that every Christian who desires to be a culture-shaper should consider living in an urban context. Then he underscores the positive role cities played in the Bible.

where you live matters **15**

"If you want to be culture-makers, you ought to live in big cities."

"One of the only things that the Greek and Roman ancient philosophers and thinkers, and the biblical writers, agreed on was that the city was the best place for human well-being, that a good city was the very best place for human flourishing."

"One of the reasons why Christianity is exploding in the non-Western world is the explosion of two-thirds world cities."

"The future is the city."

THOUGHTS

group gathering one

THE GOODNESS OF CITIES

DEBATE

Split the group into two sides* and spend fifteen minutes debating the issue:

Are cities really a good gift of God?

Record your thoughts on each position on pages 20-21.

Use the following debate starters to guide your time.

Timothy Keller makes the case that cities are an inherently good gift from God. And the Bible seems to support this perspective. But many of us have chosen not to live in urban areas. Indeed, some even represent the sentiment of famous actor Steve McQueen when he once said, "I would rather wake up in the middle of nowhere than in any city on earth." So, from your perspective, are cities really a good gift of God?

To me yes + no

DEBATE STARTERS

What compelling arguments did Timothy Keller present?

Is it possible that the negative aspects of cities (higher crime rates, poverty, crowding, etc.) outweigh the positives?

What is healthy or healthy about Steve McQueen's viewpoint?

Are there benefits to living in a suburban or rural area?

Even if you don't agree with the side you are representing, consider and offer the best arguments for your position. Be respectful.

YES

Cities are inherently good and part of God's gracious plan for humanity.

THOUGHTS

Closer to and more places to meet and see people — evangelize
closer to more people to visit me or come help me
more opportunity to meet and evangelize new people

NO

Cities tend to breed values that are contrary to God's will for our lives.

THOUGHTS

group gathering one

SEEK THE PEACE AND PROSPERITY OF THE CITY

REFLECT

Have a few people in your group take turns reading this section aloud.

Then journal your thoughts on page 25.

In the sixth century BC, the unthinkable happened to the people of Israel. After years of internal strife and external pressure, the hated Babylonian armies swept in, destroyed the great temple, and decimated Jerusalem. The king of Judah was dethroned and many of the Israelites who survived were taken captive to Babylon. The nation existed no more. As a result, the Hebrew exiles in Babylon lost all faith in God's promises. How would they ever be a great nation and a blessing to all the nations (Genesis 12:1–3) while they lived in the wicked cities of Babylon? How could Zion, the city of Jerusalem, be considered a "City of Righteousness" where "all the nations will stream to it" (Isaiah 1–2) if it lay in ruins? Their emotions tottered between great mourning and great hatred:

> By the rivers of Babylon we sat and wept
>   when we remembered Zion.
> There on the poplars
>   we hung our harps,
> for there our captors asked us for songs,
>   our tormentors demanded songs of joy;

> they said, "Sing us one of the songs of Zion!"
> How can we sing the songs of the LORD
>   while in a foreign land?
> If I forget you, Jerusalem,
>   may my right hand forget its skill.
> May my tongue cling to the roof of my mouth
>   if I do not remember you,
> if I do not consider Jerusalem
>   my highest joy.
> Remember, LORD, what the Edomites did
>   on the day Jerusalem fell.
> "Tear it down," they cried,
>   "tear it down to its foundations!"
> Daughter Babylon, doomed to destruction,
>   happy are those who repay you
>   according to what you have done to us.
> Happy are those who seize your infants
>   and dash them against the rocks.
>
> – Psalm 137

There it is—the famous verse where the Israelites' hatred was so strong that they rejoiced in the thought of Babylonian babies being dashed against the rocks. But the words of the prophet Jeremiah would challenge their entire thinking:

> This is what the LORD Almighty, the God of Israel, says to all those I carried into exile from Jerusalem to Babylon: "Build houses and settle down; plant gardens and eat what they produce. Marry and have sons and daughters; find wives for your sons and give your daughters in marriage, so that they too may have sons and

daughters. Increase in number there; do not decrease. Also, seek the peace and prosperity of the city to which I have carried you into exile. Pray to the Lord for it, because if it prospers, you too will prosper."

— Jeremiah 29:4–7

Little did they know that God had his people right where he wanted them. God had a vision for the cities of Babylon—as wicked as they were. Biblical scholar Christopher Wright explains.

> The exiles had a task—a mission no less—even in the midst of the city of their enemies. And that task was to seek the welfare of that city and to pray for the blessing of YHWH upon it. So they were not only to be the beneficiaries of God's promise to Abraham (in that they would not die out but increase), they were also to be the agents of God's promise to Abraham that through his descendants the nations would be blessed.... Let them be a blessing there to those they live among by seeking and praying for their welfare. (*The Mission of God*, InterVarsity Press, 2006, pp. 99–100)

REFLECTION STARTERS

Spend a few minutes journaling your thoughts to the two questions below. Then, share your reflections with the group.

Why do you think God instructed the exiles to build houses, settle down, plant gardens, marry, and have children? What would be the purpose or result of these specific things?

To furnish city with good by prayers, worship and more added to family to carry God to them

Think of the current place you live, whether a rural area, small town, suburb, or city. What are practical ways that you could seek its "peace and prosperity"? What would be the costs of doing so? What would be the benefits?

JOURNAL

where you live matters

SEE THE CITY AS GOD DOES

CONCLUDE

God has a heart for the city. Indeed, cities are a gift from God. Our role is to be a restorative presence in the city, and that starts with a new attitude. By seeing the city as God does, praying for the city, and seeking its prosperity, we can affect the kind of change that God desires.

How will you begin to seek the prosperity of the place where you live?

more prayer
Going about doing good to all
Speaking teaching your Word to others
praying over and for them
Driving around city and praying over places led to.

FROM THE GARDEN TO THE CITY

PREPARE FOR NEXT GATHERING

Before your next discussion, read the Q Short by Mel McGowan beginning on page 30. Be sure to set aside some uninterrupted time for this. Try not to save it until the last minute. When you read the essay, be sure to underline, highlight, or jot down comments about ideas that are particularly interesting, disconcerting, or challenging. Be prepared to share why at the next gathering.

Q SHORT

SAVING SUBURBIA: FROM THE GARDEN TO THE CITY

SAVING SUBURBIA: FROM THE GARDEN TO THE CITY
By Mel McGowan

I once lived the "American Dream."

I had a single-family detached house on a half-acre parcel with a three-car garage in a bedroom suburb of Southern California. In order to afford my piece of the "American Pie," I commuted to work at least an hour each way, barely making it home in time to tuck in my youngest child each night, and rarely in time to have dinner with the whole family. I spoke to my next-door neighbor about three times in three years. The elementary school that was located behind our tract was shut down so my son had to be driven or bussed several miles to the next school. Although I attended the same church where I became a Christian, it had long since given up its Main Street address to relocate to forty acres of agricultural land on the periphery of the city. As a result, it had achieved mega-church status, with over 5,000 weekend attendees. I felt my wife's pain as she attended week after week enjoying relevant teaching and worship, but not one real conversation, much less the start of any new friendships. It may sound like a "glass half-empty" description, but, in fact, having grown up in Europe and Asia in urban flats, apartments, and townhomes, I felt blessed to have a home like this for my family. However, something was missing from my American Dream.

I have come to understand that something to be a God-wired hunger for community.

THE KIDNAPPING OF COMMUNITY

God is a God of community. Before the beginning, the Father, Son, and Holy Spirit "did life together" in community. "In the beginning," God created a perfect setting for community—Eden—for vertical connection with him, as well as horizontal connection with others. After the cleansing of the flood, God chose a particular people—a community—to tell his story and reveal his ways. And for the past two thousand years, the Bible says that his presence has not been contained by a tent or a building but is somehow found within in Christ-centered community: the church. Humans, made in God's image and for his purposes, are hard-wired for community.

However, today, the concept of community is being kidnapped from us. To be sure, the word itself is still used at great lengths. We have special interest communities (e.g., the gay community, the evangelical community, etc.). Single-family detached tract residential builders have renamed themselves "Community Builders" and their single use tracts with the minimum required landscaped setbacks are "Master Planned Communities." And the leading Real Estate Development trade and research association, Urban Land Institute (ULI), defines "Community Centers" as a shopping center anchored by a discount or department store with a typical GLA (gross leasable area) of 150,000 to 300,000 square feet... a.k.a. a "strip center" or "big box center." But amid so much talk of community, we have lost its true meaning.

The three-car "garagescapes" that have replaced the tree-lined front porch streetscapes of small town America create anonymity and social isolation. Anonymity is also a common critique of the Sunday morning experience in the darkened rows of contemporary mega-churches (many of which actually use the word community in their name). Ironically, in order to achieve mega-church status, many of these "faith communities" are essentially once-a-week gatherings of dispersed families from the same 20-minute drive radius as a big box retail center. Given the placeless homogeneity of much suburban sprawl (the same big box retailers, tract home builders, gas stations, and "vanilla" office parks), the word seems to be invoked specifically to compensate for the lack of authentic community.

Perhaps the biggest threat to the classic definition of community is technology. The internal combustion engine killed Main Street, Elm Street, and the walkable scale of human settlements and towns. Whereas the "public square," with its sacred and civic spaces (from the Greek agora, Roman forum, and Italian piazza to the New England village green) was the first and central defining anchor to any community, for the last sixty years the creation of such public spaces is actually prohibited by modern single-use zoning practices. The latest technological shift that is radically transforming the definition of community is online social media, which seems to remove the need for actual physical spaces to connect with others. Are the "real" places becoming obsolete?

All of these changes are demonstrating that when we divorce the word *community* from the reality of a particular human-scaled place, we fundamentally lose something in the mix. Today, many church planters and next generation Christian leaders feel a calling to be "architects of *community*" in either urban or suburban settings. However, most are ill equipped to answer this call because they lack a biblical understanding of *place* and a historical understanding of terms like *city* and *suburb*. Without an adequate theology of *place*, we resort to either devaluing it (throwaway church buildings) or overdoing it (by trying to rebuild the temple). And without a greater understanding of how physical human ecologies and environments either facilitate or constrain community, we will fail to be truly present in the places and cities to which God has called us. In light of this, we'll consider a theology of place first, then explore the tangible challenges we face for creating authentic community in our cities, with a special focus on the suburbs.

A THEOLOGY OF PLACE

Some consider a theology of place to be primarily concerned with religious buildings; they focus on how to create sacred worship space. Church and religious architects would even argue that there are "timeless principles of liturgical design." I call this the standard bag of tricks. These induce the user through a series of perceptual and physiological manipulations in order to artificially induce a sense of sacred. They include using stairs and ramps for ascension, forcing the "pilgrim" to lower their head through lowered openings or ceiling elements, and then using filtered natural light to "draw the eye heavenward."

In contrast, I have come to believe that the most beautiful (not to mention opulent) cathedral can be the site of the most profane acts (e.g., child molestation), and that the smelliest back alley can be the site of the most powerful redeeming act (serving a homeless teen as if she were Jesus). A theology of place needs to be bigger than even the biggest and grandest of church buildings.

The Bible is concerned with place. Indeed, the entire biblical story can be seen as a metanarrative of the journey of God's people from one place to another, from the Garden to the City. This first place we encounter comes at the culmination of the creation story. It's a very good place.

Some of our imagery of the Garden of Eden is fuzzy, ranging from an assumption of an abstract metaphor to a literal image of an unending, unspoiled jungle. The actual word *Paradise* entered European languages from the Persian root word *pardis*, which referred to a beautifully-tended garden enclosed between walls. The Hebrew word *pardes* (probably derived from Persian and used in the Jewish Talmud to refer to Eden) could be interpreted as a park, a garden, or an orchard.

This may sound a bit off, but I find it helpful to relate the Garden of Eden to a theme park. Although an angel with a flaming sword is more impressive than a typical minimum wage theme park security guard, the idea of a carefully designed environment in which every detail (sight, sound, smell, taste, touch) is carefully considered and designed for the enjoyment of its denizens is a powerful one. In fact, it is so compelling that Disney's walled gardens are the top tourism destinations in America, Europe, and Asia. After spending nearly a decade of my life with the Walt Disney Company, I have come to appreciate the intensity and intentionality of the multi-disciplinary design effort that goes into the creation of a theme park.

However, in his book *Culture-Making*, Andy Crouch points out important differences between the Garden of Eden and the theme park.[1] He highlights that we are made in the image of God to be creative cultivators of God's creation. A theme park, with its highly scripted and choreographed experiences and environments, leaves little space for such image bearing. Rather than fulfilling our calling to be creators and cultivators, we are left with few choices other than consuming or perhaps critiquing. In contrast, God placed people in the garden of his design, commanding them to care for it, to manage, to use it, to creatively order it, and to develop it.

In light of this mandate, the Garden of Eden was a sheltered place, but it was not a perfect place. In fact, nowhere in Genesis does it say that the Garden of Eden was perfect.[2] "Perfection" generally implies "static," "fixed," or "unchanging." But in the Garden, God does something that Disney would never even think about. He leaves the people to their own devices: to use their gift of free will to do something in harmony with God's will, or to use it for their own purposes or glory—to rape, distort, abuse, and exploit it. When the wrong choice is made, creation fractures, splinters, and groans.

This story leaves us with a question and a choice of our own. Did God give up on his creation after Adam and Eve chose selfishly? The sloppy answer has been yes, that while God wants to save people from their sin, the world is "heading to hell in a handbasket." It's the notion that God has thrown in the towel on the creation that he called "good" and that "it's all gonna burn someday." Consequently, physical places here on earth are relatively insignificant, eternally speaking.

Yet, the Jewish worldview of Jesus was that not only has God not given up on creation, but that he was also actively at work within it, moving towards a rebirth, a regeneration, a renewal. Randy Alcorn—perhaps the leading theologian of heaven—articulates the biblical perspective that God will "restore everything, as he promised long ago through his holy prophets" (Acts 3:21 TNIV). He asserts, "The earth's death will be no more final than our own. The destruction of the old Earth in God's purifying judgment will immediately be followed by its resurrection to new life."[3] The Bible says that God's judgment will destroy our works of "wood, hay or straw," yet it will purify those of "gold, silver, and costly stones" (1 Cor. 3:12-15 TNIV). Moreover, the apostle John notes that when Christians die, what they have done on earth for Christ "will follow them" (Rev. 14:13 TNIV). This is why theologian Albert Wolters concludes that "those purified works on the earth must surely include the products of human culture. There is no reason to doubt that they will be transfigured and transformed by their liberation from the curse, but they will be in essential continuity with our experience now—just as our resurrected bodies, though glorified, will still be bodies."[4]

The choice then is what to do with God's creation. Like Adam and all who have followed him, we have a choice between prayerful stewardship to his glory or selfish manipulation of creation to our demise. "From the Garden to the City" could be the name of a film adaptation of the Bible; it could also refer to the first eleven chapters of Genesis, where cities become the culmination of human cultivation. Unfortunately, the stain of sin and corruption that produce the earliest cities remains indelibly etched into our perception of the city today. After Cain kills his brother Abel, he is separated from a communal relationship with God, his family, and the land. Not satisfied with God's provision of a mark of protection that will ward off those who would harm him, Cain defiantly relies on his own provision. He builds a city which functions as a surrogate form of protection and provision, similar to the way that people run away from their families and their God to the anonymity of the city today.

Genesis 1 begins with the ordering and shaping of nature, but by Genesis 11, nature is supplanted in the city of Babel. Like Cain, the residents of Babel sought to "make a name" for themselves, to control their own identity and security, and to build a "stairway to heaven" (the ziggurat form that the tower may have taken) on their own strength and to their own glory. In this city, the cultural project is the supplanting of all traces of dependence on God. What they chose to make of the world (culture) deepened their alienation and independence from their Maker. As Andy Crouch notes, "For all its moments of beauty and ingenuity, culture can easily be Babel: a fist-shaking attempt to take over God's role for ourselves."[5]

So from early in history and our reading of the Bible, the city is cast as a receptacle for sin, a "den of iniquity." However, God seems to be calling urban prophets in the tradition of Nehemiah to return, revisit, and restore the city to its rightful place as the culmination of his larger story arc. Author Eric Jacobsen even suggests that God has chosen the dense, diverse, and walkable streets of the city as a focus of redemption.[6] Just as Joseph told the brothers who had sold him into slavery "You intended to harm me, but God intended it for good" (Gen. 50:20 TNIV), God seems to be saying of our cities: "Though you meant them to be a form of escape from me, I will use them to draw you back to me." Jacobsen highlights this redemption theme throughout the cities of the Bible: Cain's desire to flee to the city after killing his brother finds a redeemed expression in the cities of refuge set apart in the Law of Moses; the fear of alienation and scattering of the citizens of Babel is redeemed when the Israelites find cities in the Promised Land in which they can gather; the desire to make a name for themselves in Babel is redeemed in the city of Jerusalem, where God causes his name to dwell. God's power to redeem is stronger than our ability to alienate and break down.

Throughout the Bible then, it becomes clear that place is important to God—whether it be wilderness or city. Although the specific geography of Israel's homeland changed (from Canaan, to Egypt, to the Wilderness, to the Promised Land, to exile, then back), his chosen people were a "place-based" community. In fact, God got pretty prescriptive with the Israelites in how he wanted everything laid out from the macro-scale of the community site plan to the micro-scale of the "smells and bells." But the end of the story culminates with the creation of another glorious place.

Just like with the Garden of Eden, God is the "architect and builder" (Heb. 11:10) of another masterfully designed environment, "the holy city, the new Jerusalem" (Rev. 21:2). Although he is the Supreme Designer of the city, God allows people to participate in the finishing of this project. This heaven (as we often call it) will be a physical place on earth where God's instruction to the first human beings is ultimately fulfilled. Besides God's own handiwork, artifacts, and people, "the glory and the honor of the nations" are brought into the city by "the kings of the earth" (Rev. 21:24-26). In this final vision of the city, it is filled with redeemed human culture. The question of what cultural artifacts will make it into the New Jerusalem is a fascinating one. Andy Crouch doesn't bet on "cultural mediocrity, the half-baked and half-hearted efforts to make something of the world." He does bet on certain works of Bach, Miles Davis, green tea crème brulee, fish tacos, *Moby Dick*, *The Odyssey*, and the iPod, while recognizing that they would be suitably purified and redeemed, like our resurrected bodies.[7]

C. S. Lewis imaginatively conveyed the continuity of the Old and New Earth in this passage from *The Last Battle*:

The difference between the old Narnia and the new Narnia was ...

The new one was a deeper country: every rock and flower and blade of grass looked as if it meant more ...

"The reason why we loved the old Narnia is that it sometimes looked a little like this"...

"Why!" exclaimed Peter. "It's England. And that's the house itself—Professor Kirk's old home in the country where all our adventures began!"

"I thought that house had been destroyed," said Edmund.

"So it was," said the Faun. "But you are now looking at the England within England, the real England just as this is the real Narnia. And in that inner England no good thing is destroyed."[8]

As an architectural/urban designer, I am a card-carrying member of the Supreme Architect's fan club. The common thread in design that stands the test of time—that takes into consideration this theology of place in both the Garden and the City—is not traditionalism, functionalism, minimalism, or the avant garde. It is working with, not against God's architecture, whether it is the natural topography, native ecology, prevailing wind patterns, or solar orientation. We should draw inspiration from, rather than ignore or compete with, his creation. This is true whether the designer acknowledges the authorship of a Creator or not. It is the thread that holds together the local vernacular architecture that inspires a luxury resort in Bali, Mont St. Michel, a National Park lodge, the Arts & Crafts movement, Louis Sullivan, Frank Lloyd Wright, Frank Gehry's organic structural sculptures, and George Lucas' depiction of the capital of "Naboo." Personally, I wouldn't be surprised to find not only works of fine architecture, but also my grandparent's mountain cabin on the other side of eternity.

This realization has changed everything in my approach to community design and architecture. The idea that a site plan could be prayerfully considered, rather than seen as a simple technical solution or a functional diagram, has revolutionized my design philosophy. But what about the average Christian? What does a theology of place have to do with our everyday lives? *Everything*.

The God of Place did not teach that true spirituality is about eventually escaping this world to some other place in the sky where we will live forever. A Christian should anticipate spending forever here, in a new City of Heaven that comes to a renewed Earth. Rob Bell puts it this way:

Jesus wants his followers to bring heaven, not hell, to earth. This has been God's intention for people since the beginning... The entire movement of the Bible is of a God who wants to be here, with his people. The church is described later as being the temple of God. And how does the Bible end? With God "coming down" and taking up residence here on earth. The goal isn't escaping the world but making this world the kind of place God can come to. And God is remaking us into the kind of people who can do this kind of work.[9]

If we take this seriously, does it change the houses that we buy, the neighborhoods we live in, the places we shop, and the products that we consume? Definitely. Perhaps most challenged is our pursuit of the American Dream. Let's take a closer look.

AUTOPIA

One of the top current television shows is the phenomenon known as *American Idol*. As people across the country, including many Christians, root for their favorite Idol, two ironies strike me. The obvious irony is the full embrace, even worship, of the show, its participants, and its brand by those who profess a Judeo-Christian faith, in the face of the Second Commandment. The other, more subtle, irony is the obliviousness of our worship of the true American Idol—the suburban American Dream—and the damage it has caused to our lives and the sacredness of place.

A brief survey of history reveals that human ecologies and communities have certain consistencies and patterns that have repeated themselves across space and time. Up until the twentieth century, people throughout history lived in human-scaled environments, defined largely by the radius and distance that a person could walk. Building heights were also limited by the number of stairs a person could comfortably climb. A diversity of uses made it possible to live, work, learn, and play within a reasonable distance of each other, if not on top of each other. Finally, various densities of homes allowed multiple generations of families to live in the same community, if they so chose. Then something fundamentally changed.

A new technology called the internal combustion engine radically transformed the scale of living. For thousands of years, a twenty-minute commute meant a one-mile radius for most, which was the characteristic size of some of the largest cities. The car created a new regional scale in which people could live, work, and play twenty miles or more from each destination. At the same time and partly as a result, Modernism took root in both architecture and community planning, united by the dictum that "form follows function." Many of the first generation European Modern architects took this as an opportunity to rid architecture of its potential to communicate the values, culture, and faith of a community. Since many felt that religion was an "opium of the masses," they stripped buildings of the gargoyles, buttresses, and iconography. The reason that this movement flourished had less to do with the public adoptions of this anti-theology (CBD) as a result of single-use functional zoning. Urban design evolved with the City Beautiful movement and almost a sole focus on creating grand civic and governmental centers. Once these areas were stripped of homes, schools, and churches, retail departed as well.

CRACKS IN THIS VERSION OF THE AMERICAN DREAM ARE GETTING HARDER TO HIDE.

and more to do with the fact that it took much less skill, cost, and time to produce "functional boxes." The real damage was done by Modernist planners whose functionalist approach led to zoning, in which a community is broken up into specific functional zones: residential (of various densities), retail, office park, industrial, etc. The combination of the automobile and new Modernism was a death knell to human-scaled community.

This combination, however, proved a potent facilitator of a new American Dream. For the first time in human history, the "city" (regardless of scale) was no longer viewed as the proper and safe container of community. "Downtown" became synonymous with the "Central Business District"

Partially in response to the dehumanization of the Industrial Revolution, environmental designers including Andrew Jackson Downing, Frederick Law Olmstead, Ebenezer Howard, and Frank Lloyd Wright began articulating a competing, yet complementary vision to the high-rise urban vision of European architectural modernists. What they effectively argued was that we should "return" to the garden, and create a new suburban landscape. The original "garden city" models of the late nineteenth and early twentieth century were promising. They were intricately planned around natural features and emulated the scale and organic feel of a medieval village, with a rich variety of housing types and uses. Many of these communities (e.g., Mariemont, Ohio; Riverside, Illinois; Forest Hills

Gardens, New York; Country Club District, Missouri; Beverly Hills, California) remain some of the most prized communities in the nation. And many were based on a walkable radius to a rail transit station.

Following World War II, the American Dream machine kicked into full gear. Seemingly unrelated federal government initiatives changed the face of the nation. President Eisenhower, impressed with the German Autobahn system, pushed forward the Federal Aid Highway Act in 1956. Appropriating $25 billion for the construction of 41,000 miles of the Interstate system over a twenty-year period, it was the largest public works project in American history to that point. Although done in the name of military defense (the technical name was the National Interstate and Defense Highways Act), the most direct result of the act was the government's subsidization of suburban sprawl, making commutes between urban centers to suburbs much quicker and furthering the flight of citizens and businesses and divestment from inner cities. A secondary result was the tearing up of any alternative urban transportation systems (e.g., the elimination of Los Angeles' extensive interurban railway system as funded by auto-related industries).

On the housing front, the government heavily incentivized the home ownership of suburban detached homes through the widespread availability of mortgages (through the Veterans Administration and the Federal Housing Administration) as well as mortgage interest deduction. Somehow in the process we went from being able to build our own custom or Sears catalog "kit" home and have it paid off in three to five years, to the situation we find ourselves in today, in which thirty years of interest payments are the norm and millions of homes are in or face foreclosure. These trends along with lax underwriting standards have encouraged the median home size in America to become 2400 square feet, compared to 800 square feet in the UK and the European Union.

One fundamental departure from historical urbanity within the "antiurban" suburban model is the attempt to freeze time. Historically, any human settlement has been allowed to grow organically and mature in response to changing demographic, environmental, and economic demands. As the American "Leave it to Beaver" home was elevated to the status of an unquestioned dream, housing subdivisions created more elaborate Covenant, Codes, & Restrictions and Homeowner's Association design guidelines to ensure that the status quo would remain forever. Ironically however, the other supportive land uses that followed the government subsidies and new freeways (strip malls, office/industrial parks, and even institutions) seemed to adopt and embrace a transient or temporal model: "throwaway" architecture in the name of minimalism, functionalism, or more honestly, cheapness. Pre-engineered metal industrial buildings, stick-built stucco prototype retail stores, and warehouse churches are standard in suburbia. Again, these are not simply aesthetic decisions. Financing models embraced by commercial lenders encourage lower construction costs, while governmental tax policies encourage faster depreciation of physical assets.

This is the reality of Autopia. And if you haven't noticed, cracks in this version of the American Dream are getting harder to hide. People are tired of spending a quarter tank of gasoline to buy a quart of milk. Only 10 percent of kids have a school they can walk to. After our long commutes, we pull into our three-car garage and enter the kitchen door without ever talking to our neighbors. We have little genuine community. Yet we think we have the home we want. Indeed, Americans have shown an amazing willingness to continue to extend their commute time in order to qualify for the home that they want. But as negative equity situations and foreclosures rise, some have questioned the viability of this version of the American Dream.

For starters, Autopia no longer fits our context. The American Dream machine has been focused on one demographic: married with children. With the aging of Baby Boomers, later marriages, and fewer children, less than a third of new US households formed are forecasted to fit this demographic! Many suburban church plants and mega-churches have almost exclusively focused on this demographic. One forecast states that the current glut of single family detached homes will not meet their anticipated demand until 2030. Gen "Next," empty nesters, young urban professionals, and DINKs (Double-Income No Kids) are increasingly showing a preference for diversity over monotony in choosing more "urbane" live/work/play settings. Studies consistently show a willingness to pay a premium for smaller lots or properties if they are located within access to transit and/or have features of a "New Urbanist" community.

Second, Autopia no longer works. Various proclamations, from President Obama to the Urban Land Institute, have stated that the era of building sprawl is over. The biggest reasons have less to do with "consumer preference" or lifestyle choice, but with economics and the environment. Even young couples with children prefer foreclosure-resistant neighborhoods where transportation costs are low (about 9 percent of household expenditures) rather than foreclosure-risky neighborhoods in the outer suburbs where transportation costs are high (25 percent or more of household expenditures). According to a 2000 Impact Analysis for the Georgia Regional Transportation Authority, a suburban resident of Atlanta is likely to drive an average of eight times more miles than an urban resident. Low-density suburban development results in the highest per capita demands on natural systems and habitats, including impervious land cover, miles driven, water use, energy use, air pollution, and greenhouse gas production. Issues of energy availability (the near-term global prospect of peaking oil supply no longer being able to keep up with global demand) and the changing regulatory context of climate change (whether you believe in it or not) is making the cost of getting access to raw land and serving greenfield development higher and higher.

CREATING SACRED SPACE IN SUBURBIA

In my work, I have a lot of conversations about the future of the church with many established and emerging Christian leaders and pastors. One trend I have noticed is a tendency toward false dichotomies. Suburban is out, urban is in. The mega-church campus is out, while the multi-site alternative and church plants are in. I find some of these generalizations a bit troubling. As architects of the next generation of Christian community, I believe that pastors and church planters need to have a richer understanding of the emerging postmodern landscape. For the first time in human history, the UN estimates that half of the world's 6.7 billion people are living in urban areas. This does not mean that half of humanity is crammed in high-rise towers in a Central Business District. In fact "Downtown" residents of major metro areas only represent around 2 percent of total households. More accurate definitions of "urban" and official jurisdictional boundaries of "cities" (as opposed to the classic definition as a walkable, dense, diverse settlement) fully incorporate the suburban periphery into their scope. For example, most of the Northeastern corridor of the US incorporating Boston, New York, Philadelphia, Baltimore, and Washington, D.C. is considered urbanized according to the UN statistic.

So suburbia is part of the city.

Can it be retrofitted to meet the needs of emerging demographics and the God-wired hunger for community? Can a theology of place exist in Autopia? A movement of planners, government leaders, and architects called the Congress for New Urbanism has demonstrated over the past few decades how "urbanity" can be inserted not only back into major urban cores, but also in suburban city and town centers by taming the car. Rather than building with the assumption that everyone will arrive by car and park separately for each use, we have learned how to "stash" parking in the rear of buildings, on-streets, and in garages. Rather than separating the different land uses miles from each other (as modernist zoning did), we have learned (or relearned) how to stack multi-family or office space above retail to create active streetscapes that frame outdoor rooms. Former greyfield (parking lots), brownfield (industrial sites), and obsolete retail malls are being redeveloped as vibrant centers within the generic field of suburban sprawl. Unfortunately, what hasn't been widely understood is how to integrate sacred space and Christian community into the mix.

Just as God called Nehemiah back to restore the city of God, I believe that God is calling Christians today to redeem and restore sustainable Christ-centered community back to the heart of our communities, even where endless agglomerations of suburban subdivisions have never previously had a heart. Every believer can start by following Christ's command to "love your neighbor" and taking the "neighbor" thing a little more seriously. Don't settle for a placeless metaphor instead of real community. A neighborhood barbecue is a start. Too many Christians have grown so accustomed to their fellowship with the "equally yoked" that the thought of a neighbor showing up with a cooler of beer sends shivers up their spine. Love someone enough that you still want to be a part of their life if they never go to church!

Choosing your neighborhood is choosing a mission field; prayerfully consider God's leading in the same way that a missionary would. This singular decision is also the one that will have the greatest impact on our creation care footprint. The choice of where we live in relation to daily life needs: work, school, the grocery store, etc. is the single biggest variable with influence on the economic and environmental sustainability of our communities. One simple benchmark is Walkability.[10] The energy savings and carbon footprint of intelligently sited and integrated neighborhoods that are walkable has been well documented.

Churches can consider their place in the city by defining their community beyond their property lines. In many cases, rather than being an "anchor," an "asset," or a "heart" of the neighborhood (as it used to be), churches are perceived as a NIMBY (Not-In-My-Backyard) undesirable use because of the property and sales tax drain and off-site parking and traffic concerns. For the past half-decade I have been engaged in various experiments in integrating faith communities back into the fabric of community cores and what I call Postmodern Agoras. Here are some various strategies for churches to consider:

1. Develop surplus acreage of surface parking lots into mixed-use community buildings that create a "drawbridge" to the community.

2. Recast churches as performing arts or community centers that are more readily recognized as "anchors" for retail or town center development.

3. Pursue joint-development strategies with mixed-use/new town developers which reserve ministry building pads, while minimizing the amount of dedicated Sunday morning parking required (e.g., sharing office/retail parking spaces).

4. Redevelop obsolete retail/big-box anchors and centers as "Main Streets" or church-anchored "piazzas."

The challenge can sometimes seem daunting: to create sacred space in the heart(s) of the city, even in the heart of Autopia; to bring a bit of the kingdom of heaven to earth; to build something that just might last the trial by fire. May you follow the God of Nehemiah on the journey to real community.

Mel McGowan is President and Founder of Visioneering Studios, a national architecture, urban planning, and interior design firm with offices in Irvine, Denver, and Atlanta. His background includes film, urban design, and a decade-long stint with the Walt Disney Company. Visioneering recently received the 2009 Solomon Award for "Best Church Architect." Mel speaks extensively on sustainable Christ-centered community and is the author of Design Like God Gives a Damn: Revolutionizing Sacred Space (2009).

END NOTES

[1] Andy Crouch, *Culture Making: Recovering Our Creative Calling* (Downers Grove: InterVarsity Press, 2008), 112.

[2] Rob Bell, *Velvet Elvis: Repainting the Christian Faith* (Grand Rapids: Zondervan, 2005), 158.

[3] Randy Alcorn, *Heaven* (Wheaton: Tyndale House Publishers, 2004), 357.

[4] Albert Wolters, *Creation Regained: Biblical Basics for a Reformational Worldview* (Grand Rapids: Eerdmans, 1985), 41.

[5] Crouch, *Culture Making*, 117.

[6] Eric O. Jacobsen, *Sidewalks in the Kingdom: New Urbanism and the Christian Faith* (Grand Rapids: Brazos Press, 2003), 44.

[7] Crouch, *Culture Making*, 170.

[8] C. S. Lewis, *The Last Battle* (New York: Collier Books, 1956), 171-181.

[9] Bell, *Velvet Elvis*, 149-150.

[10] See the "Walk Score" of any property at http://www.walkscore.com

City life is millions of people being lonesome together.

HENRY DAVID THOREAU

Slums may well be breeding grounds of crime, but middle-class suburbs are incubators of apathy and delirium.

CYRIL CONNOLLY

The peace of the celestial city is the perfectly ordered and harmonious enjoyment of God, and of one another in God.

AUGUSTINE

GROUP GATHERING TWO
FROM THE GARDEN TO THE CITY

LIVING IN THE SUBURBS

DISCUSS

Suburbia is a relatively new phenomenon in the Western world. And many of us have experienced its lifestyle firsthand.

DISCUSSION STARTERS

Have you ever lived in a suburban context?

What are the strengths of living in the suburbs? Weaknesses?

In your experience, how are the characteristics of living in a suburb similar or different to what Mel McGowan described?

COMMUNITY SATISFACTION

LEVELS OF COMMUNITY SATISFACTION

	HIGH	MEDIUM	LOW
Cities	34%	36%	30%
SUBURBS	**42%**	**33%**	**25%**
Small towns	25%	38%	37%
Rural areas	29%	35%	36%

IF YOU COULD LIVE ANYWHERE, WHAT WOULD YOU PREFER?

City	23%
Suburb	25%
SMALL TOWNS	**30%**
Rural areas	21%
DK/Refused	1%

Source: Pew Research Center Social & Demographic Trends Study: "Suburbs Not Most Popular, But Suburbanites Most Content" by Richard Morin and Paul Taylor, February 26, 2009 at http://pewsocialtrends.org/pubs/727/content-in-american-suburbs.

OUR WORKS BRING ETERNAL RESTORATION

DEBATE

Split the group into two sides* and spend twenty minutes debating the issue:

Do our physical works and accomplishments endure eternally?

Record your thoughts on each position on pages 50-51.

Use the following debate starters to guide your time.

In his Q Short, Mel McGowan asserts that Christians should have a more robust "theology of place." He also argues that we shouldn't take the approach to our current world—the cities we build and the good things we contribute toward them—that "it's all gonna burn someday." Rather, what we create and do today that brings goodness and restoration to our cities will endure in eternity (see page 32). Is this really true? Do our physical works and accomplishments endure eternally?

DEBATE STARTERS

In a million years, what will be more important: the time we spent improving our neighborhoods and cities, or the time we spent telling others about Jesus?

Did Jesus die on the cross and rise from the grave to save people from their sins or is there more to it than that?

The Old Testament seems to place a high priority on things like taking good care of the land and the aesthetics of the temple. Does this have any relevance?

When Jesus returns, will he destroy this world and create a new one, or will he transform this existing world into a new and recreated one?

Even if you don't agree with the side you are representing, consider and offer the best arguments for your position. Be respectful.

YES

Our physical works and accomplishments have eternal significance.

THOUGHTS

NO

We live in a decaying world and should be much more focused on the destiny of people's souls.

THOUGHTS

group gathering two

THE PARADIGMATIC PLACE

REFLECT

Have a few people in your group take turns reading this section aloud.

Then journal your thoughts on pages 57-59.

Mel McGowan makes the point that the story of the Bible moves "from the Garden to the City." God's people have always found their place in the larger story by embracing their purpose in and to the physical places they have been called. It began in the Garden, and after Adam and Eve's rebellion and exile, God continued to call his people to significant places: Abraham to the land of Canaan, Moses to Mount Sinai, Israel to the wilderness, and Paul to Asia Minor and Europe. But more often than not, those significant places included cities. And no city represents God's will for his people more than their final destination: the New Jerusalem.

Interestingly, this mysterious city is not only described in the book of Revelation. Throughout the prophetic writings of the Old Testament are messages about God's ultimate vision for ancient Jerusalem. As we discovered in the previous group gathering, the Babylonians destroyed the ancient city of Jerusalem in 586 BC (it would be destroyed by the Romans again in AD 70). But through the Old Testament prophets, God painted a picture of a New Jerusalem, a restored Jerusalem, a paradigmatic place that would embody God's intentions for humanity and his creation.

Take about fifteen minutes for several people to read aloud the following extended passages from Isaiah and Revelation. As you listen, underline those phrases or sentences that stick out the most. At first, the Isaiah passage appears to be about the nation of Israel, the people, or maybe even the Messiah. But it soon becomes clear that God's Perfect City is in view.

> "Arise, shine, for your light has come,
>   and the glory of the Lord rises upon you.
>   See, darkness covers the earth
>   and thick darkness is over the peoples,
> but the Lord rises upon you
>   and his glory appears over you.
>   Nations will come to your light,
>   and kings to the brightness of your dawn.
> "Foreigners will rebuild your walls,
>   and their kings will serve you.
> Though in anger I struck you,
>   in favor I will show you compassion.
> Your gates will always stand open,
>   they will never be shut, day or night,
> so that people may bring you the wealth of the nations—
>   their kings led in triumphal procession.
> For the nation or kingdom that will not serve you will perish;
>   it will be utterly ruined.
> "The glory of Lebanon will come to you,
>   the juniper, the fir and the cypress together,
> to adorn my sanctuary;
>   and I will glorify the place for my feet.
> The children of your oppressors will come bowing before you;

    all who despise you will bow down at your feet
and will call you the City of the Lord,
    Zion of the Holy One of Israel.

"Although you have been forsaken and hated,
    with no one traveling through,
I will make you the everlasting pride
    and the joy of all generations.
You will drink the milk of nations
    and be nursed at royal breasts.
Then you will know that I, the Lord, am your Savior,
    your Redeemer, the Mighty One of Jacob.
Instead of bronze I will bring you gold,
    and silver in place of iron.
Instead of wood I will bring you bronze,
    and iron in place of stones.
I will make peace your governor
    and well-being your ruler.
No longer will violence be heard in your land,
    nor ruin or destruction within your borders,
but you will call your walls Salvation
    and your gates Praise.
The sun will no more be your light by day,
    nor will the brightness of the moon shine on you,
for the Lord, will be your everlasting light,
    and your God will be your glory.
Your sun will never set again,
    and your moon will wane no more;
the Lord, will be your everlasting light,
    and your days of sorrow will end.
Then will all your people be righteous
    and they will possess the land forever.

> They are the shoot I have planted,
>   the work of my hands,
>   for the display of my splendor.
> The least of you will become a thousand,
>   the smallest a mighty nation.
> I am the Lord;
>   in its time I will do this swiftly."
>
> – Isaiah 60:1–4, 10–22

In the book of Revelation, the apostle John receives a vision of God's consummation of history:

> Then I saw "a new heaven and a new earth," for the first heaven and the first earth had passed away, and there was no longer any sea. I saw the Holy City, the new Jerusalem, coming down out of heaven from God, prepared as a bride beautifully dressed for her husband. And I heard a loud voice from the throne saying, "Look! God's dwelling place is now among the people, and he will dwell with them. They will be his people, and God himself will be with them and be their God. 'He will wipe every tear from their eyes. There will be no more death' or mourning or crying or pain, for the old order of things has passed away."
>
> And [an angel] carried me away in the Spirit to a mountain great and high, and showed me the Holy City, Jerusalem, coming down out of heaven from God. It shone with the glory of God, and its brilliance was like that of a very precious jewel, like a jasper, clear as crystal. It had a great, high wall with twelve gates, and with twelve angels at the gates. On the gates were written the names of the twelve tribes of Israel. There were three gates on the east, three on the north,

three on the south and three on the west. The wall of the city had twelve foundations, and on them were the names of the twelve apostles of the Lamb.

I did not see a temple in the city, because the Lord God Almighty and the Lamb are its temple. The city does not need the sun or the moon to shine on it, for the glory of God gives it light, and the Lamb is its lamp. The nations will walk by its light, and the kings of the earth will bring their splendor into it. On no day will its gates ever be shut, for there will be no night there. The glory and honor of the nations will be brought into it. Nothing impure will ever enter it, nor will anyone who does what is shameful or deceitful, but only those whose names are written in the Lamb's book of life.

Then the angel showed me the river of the water of life, as clear as crystal, flowing from the throne of God and of the Lamb down the middle of the great street of the city. On each side of the river stood the tree of life, bearing twelve crops of fruit, yielding its fruit every month. And the leaves of the tree are for the healing of the nations. No longer will there be any curse. The throne of God and of the Lamb will be in the city, and his servants will serve him. They will see his face, and his name will be on their foreheads. There will be no more night. They will not need the light of a lamp or the light of the sun, for the Lord God will give them light. And they will reign for ever and ever.

– Revelation 21:1–4, 10–14, 22–27; 22:1–5

REFLECTION STARTERS

Spend a few minutes journaling your thoughts to the three questions below. Then, share your reflections with the group.

What do these two descriptions from Isaiah and Revelation have in common?

What kinds of values characterize the New Jerusalem?

What values exist in our current cities that are not present in this city?

JOURNAL

JOURNAL

JOURNAL

PLACE IS IMPORTANT

CONCLUDE

Geographic places are important in the Bible. And none is more important than New Jerusalem: a picture of the kind of place that God created us for. By understanding God's intentions for the places where we live, we can more effectively be his instruments to creating those kinds of places today.

How will you begin to consider where you live through the lens of a "theology of place"?

OUR OPPORTUNITY IN THE SUBURBS

PREPARE FOR NEXT GATHERING

Before your next discussion, set aside one hour to explore your neighborhood. You can walk the streets, ride a bike, or drive in your car through the streets of your immediate neighborhood (don't go more than a couple of miles from your residence). On a piece of paper or electronic device, record the biggest needs that you perceive. What is in need of restoration? Be prepared to share your list with the group.

PREPARING FOR YOUR CULTURE SHAPING PROJECT

In the next few weeks, your group will take part in a project together to apply what you are learning and discussing. It's important that you complete this project before your last gathering. Three options for what your group can do have been recommended on pages 96-97. All of them require some planning and preparation. Take a few minutes now to read the options and discuss which one best suits your group. You don't have to make a decision this week, but you need to get the ball rolling and be prepared to make a decision and start planning at your next group meeting.

Suburbia is where the developer bulldozes out the trees, then names the streets after [those trees].

BILL VAUGHN

Los Angeles is 72 suburbs in search of a city.

DOROTHY PARKER

GROUP GATHERING THREE
THE FUTURE OF THE SUBURBS

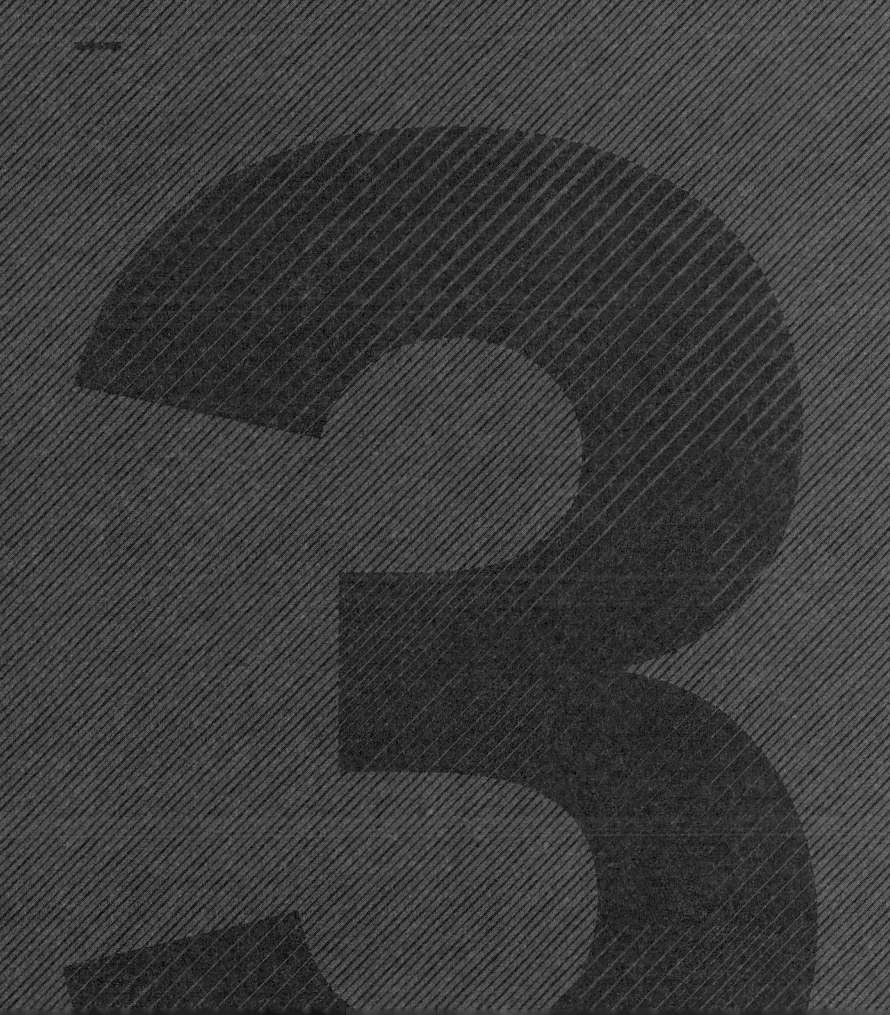

group gathering three

YOUR NEIGHBORHOOD

DISCUSS

Since your last group gathering, you had the opportunity to explore your immediate neighborhood. Much of it may have been familiar. But perhaps you noticed some buildings, people, or needs that you had never seen before. Maybe something stood out that calls for your attention.

DISCUSSION STARTERS

Were you surprised by anything you saw?

What were the greatest needs you observed?

Whose responsibility is it to address these needs?

What role could you or your community of faith play in responding?

"JUST HOW WOULD YOU DEFINE 'NEIGHBOR'?"

JESUS ANSWERED BY TELLING A STORY. "THERE WAS ONCE A MAN TRAVELING FROM JERUSALEM TO JERICHO. ON THE WAY HE WAS ATTACKED BY ROBBERS. THEY TOOK HIS CLOTHES, BEAT HIM UP, AND WENT OFF LEAVING HIM HALF-DEAD. LUCKILY, A PRIEST WAS ON HIS WAY DOWN THE SAME ROAD, BUT WHEN HE SAW HIM HE ANGLED ACROSS TO THE OTHER SIDE. THEN A LEVITE RELIGIOUS MAN SHOWED UP; HE ALSO AVOIDED THE INJURED MAN.

"A SAMARITAN TRAVELING THE ROAD CAME ON HIM. WHEN HE SAW THE MAN'S CONDITION, HIS HEART WENT OUT TO HIM. HE GAVE HIM FIRST AID, DISINFECTING AND BANDAGING HIS WOUNDS. THEN HE LIFTED HIM ONTO HIS DONKEY, LED HIM TO AN INN, AND MADE HIM COMFORTABLE. IN THE MORNING HE TOOK OUT TWO SILVER COINS AND GAVE THEM TO THE INNKEEPER, SAYING, 'TAKE GOOD CARE OF HIM. IF IT COSTS ANY MORE, PUT IT ON MY BILL—I'LL PAY YOU ON MY WAY BACK.'

"WHAT DO YOU THINK? WHICH OF THE THREE BECAME A NEIGHBOR TO THE MAN ATTACKED BY ROBBERS?"

"THE ONE WHO TREATED HIM KINDLY," THE RELIGION SCHOLAR RESPONDED. JESUS SAID, "GO AND DO THE SAME."

– LUKE 10:29-37 (MSG)

group gathering three

THE FUTURE OF THE SUBURBS

WATCH

View Q Talk: The Future of the Suburbs by Joel Kotkin

Record your thoughts on the talk on page 69.

Joel Kotkin is a noted author, futurist, and Presidential Fellow in Urban Futures at Chapman University. He is an internationally recognized authority on global, economic, political, and social trends.

At Q Austin, Joel Kotkin presented about the emergence of suburbia in the twentieth century and its impact on American life. He also asserted, in light of numerous recent statistics, that the suburbs will continue to represent the largest area of growth over the next several decades.

where you live matters 67

"[The suburbs] had roots with the Protestant churches [in early twentieth-century England] trying to figure out how they could make life better for the people who were living in these dense, industrial cities."

"If you're thinking about your churches and where your churches are going to be in the future, [the suburbs] are where most of the growth is going to take place."

"The future of suburbia is more diversity and the return of the multi-generational neighborhood."

"The suburbs need a sense of identity. . . . Historically, cities are made up of three things: the sacred, the safe, and the busy. . . . What's been missing [from the suburbs] is the sense of the sacred."

THOUGHTS

where you live matters

SUBURBAN CHURCHES ARE PART OF THE PROBLEM

DEBATE

Split the group into two sides* and spend fifteen minutes debating the issue:

Is the church contributing to the problem of the suburbs missing a sense of identity and the sacred?

Record your thoughts on each position on pages 72-73.

Use the following debate starters to guide your time.

Joel Kotkin shared several statistics in his talk:

- Between 2000 and 2006, about 92 percent of metropolitan growth was in the suburbs.
- About 50 percent of all immigrants now move to the suburbs.
- In the next 40 years, up to 80 million more people will move into the suburbs or small towns.

Clearly, the suburbs will continue to grow. But Joel Kotkin also noted that the suburbs are currently missing a sense of identity and the sacred. Is the church contributing to this problem?

DEBATE STARTERS

Can suburban culture really be transformed by a church?

Does the geography of the suburbs make it impossible for churches to restore a central place in the neighborhood and a sense of identity and sacredness?

How would suburban churches need to change in order to make a greater impact on the community?

Is it really a value for suburban churches to have a presence in the community, or should they focus on meeting the individual needs of their attendees?

*Even if you don't agree with the side you are representing, consider and offer the best arguments for your position. Be respectful.

group gathering three

YES

Suburban churches contribute to the negative aspects of the suburbs through characteristics such as their unimaginative architecture, consumer-driven mentality, and lack of diversity.

THOUGHTS

NO

Suburban churches are merely representing the culture of the suburbs and doing the best they can to minister to people there.

THOUGHTS

A PARTICULAR MISSION

REFLECT

Journal your thoughts to the following questions, then share with the group.

Joel Kotkin is hopeful about the future of the suburbs and the church's role within them. He stated, "The church has a particular mission in the suburbs." How would you define that mission?

REFLECTION STARTERS

What is unique about the suburbs that makes the church's mission there unique?

If you could describe the church's mission in the suburbs in one sentence, what would it be?

JOURNAL

OUR OPPORTUNITY IN THE SUBURBS

CONCLUDE

The suburbs are important too. They are flourishing in American culture, but they are also lacking a sacred presence. The church has a unique opportunity if only we will seize it.

What is your responsibility in helping your local church discern its role in your community?

GRACE IN AND FOR THE CITY

PREPARE FOR NEXT GATHERING

Set aside about thirty minutes to read the book of 1 Peter in your Bible. This letter was written to Christians in the first century, "scattered exiles" in the cities of the Roman Empire. There are various instructions in the letter about living a holy life, following Christ's example, and enduring suffering. But read the letter through the lens of where you live. What instructions speak directly to how Christian should live in their cities and neighborhoods in the midst of so many others who do not share their faith?

Spend the final portion of your time together discussing your culture shaping project.

PLANNING THE CULTURE SHAPING PROJECT

You'll need to make a decision by the end of this gathering since what you do will likely require planning. Your project needs to take place before your last group gathering and it should be something that everyone can participate in. You can review the suggestions given on pages 96-97. It may be difficult to find total agreement among the group, but try to establish some consensus by talking through the advantages and disadvantages of all suggestions. Don't be afraid to think creatively and challenge yourselves. You're not limited by the suggestions included in this study, but you'll want to undertake something that will help you apply what you've been learning. Make a decision and solidify action steps before you conclude.

The community finally composed of several villages is the city-state; it has at last attained the limit of virtually complete self-sufficiency, and thus, while it comes into existence for the sake of life, it exists for the good life.

ARISTOTLE

Early Christianity was primarily an urban movement.

RODNEY STARK

It was in the cities of the Roman Empire that Christianity, though born in the village culture of Palestine, had its greatest successes.

C. S. LEWIS

GROUP GATHERING FOUR
GRACE IN AND FOR THE CITY

group gathering four

REEXAMINING THE URBAN CENTER

DISCUSS

Our discussion will now come full circle. Even though there is a place for Christians in the suburbs, small towns, and even rural areas, it's no secret that urban centers are the heart of American culture. And many people are choosing to move there.

DISCUSSION STARTERS

How would your life change if you were to move into the heart of an urban area (e.g., Manhattan, Chicago, etc.)?

What would be the challenges?

What would be the rewards?

where you live matters   **81**

WHERE DO YOU LIVE?

WHERE DO YOU LIVE NOW?

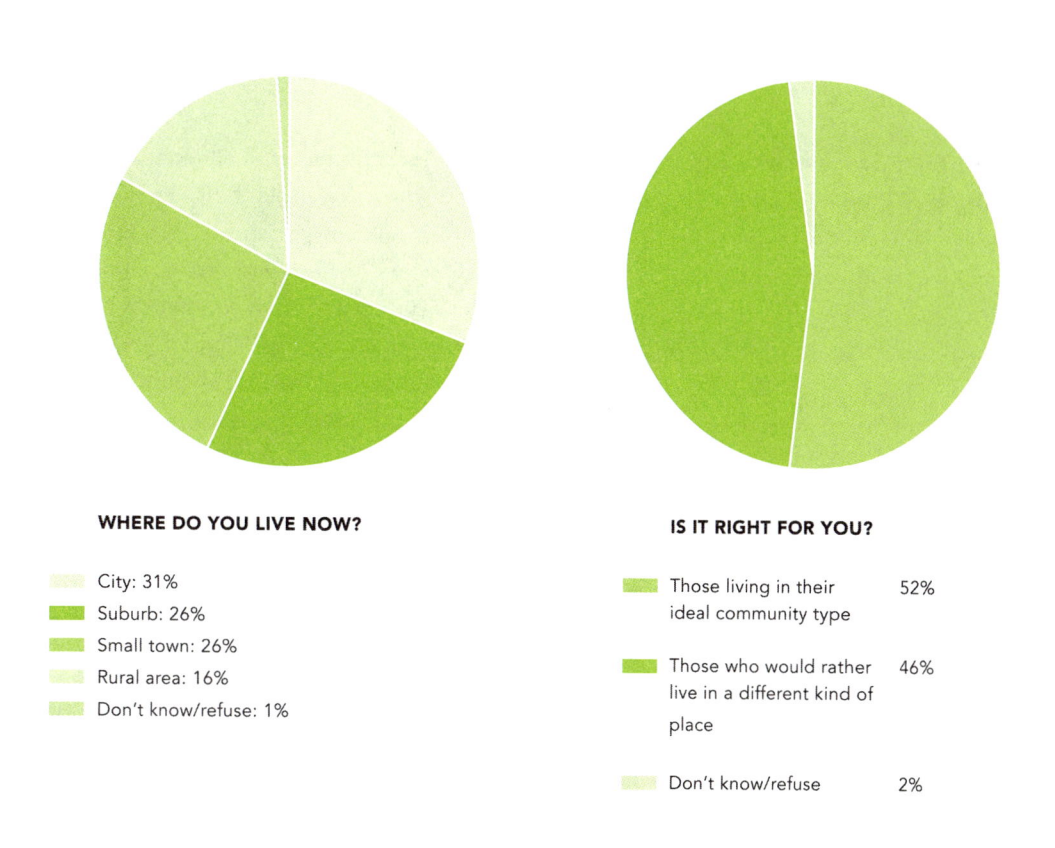

- City: 31%
- Suburb: 26%
- Small town: 26%
- Rural area: 16%
- Don't know/refuse: 1%

IS IT RIGHT FOR YOU?

- Those living in their ideal community type — 52%
- Those who would rather live in a different kind of place — 46%
- Don't know/refuse — 2%

Source: Pew Research Center Social & Demographic Trends Study: "For Nearly Half of America, Grass Is Greener Somewhere Else; Denver Tops List of Favorite Cities," January 29, 2009 at http://pewsocialtrends.org/pubs/722/grass-greener-somewhere-else-top-cities.

group gathering four

GRACE IN AND FOR THE CITY

WATCH

View Q Talk: Grace in and for the City by Timothy Keller.

Record your thoughts on the talk on page 85.

At Q New York, Timothy Keller challenged Christian leaders to reconsider where they live in light of God's heart for cities. In the first part of his talk (viewed in the first group gathering), he contended that every Christian who desires to be a culture-shaper should consider living in an urban context. In this second part of his talk, he defines the nature of a "city" as opposed to a suburban context and challenges Christians to consider the benefits of living, working, and ministering in the city.

where you live matters **83**

"What's a city? Today, when you and I think of city, we think a city as a place of large population. But that's not the way the Bible or ancient people described it. A city is a mixed-use, walkable human settlement. And if you have those two characteristics, then two more follow: a place of density and diversity."

"What suburbs do is they destroy the idea of a city completely."

"When Jesus Christ finishes his work and creates a society under God, we get to Revelation and we see that what he produces is a city. It's not just a city; it's the Garden of Eden, developed the way it was supposed to be developed, now with music, now with bridges, now with gardens, now with stories. That's the reason why even under the fallenness of our condition, cities are the place where culture happens."

"If you want to come to the city, it's a hard place to come. If you're really going to make a dent here, you need the grace of love."

THOUGHTS

group gathering four

CITIES VS. SUBURBS

DEBATE

Split the group into two sides* and spend fifteen minutes debating the issue:

Can Christians make a bigger impact in this world when they live in cities?

Record your thoughts on each position on pages 88-89.

Use the following debate starters to guide your time.

In the last group gathering, we discussed the opportunity the church has for bringing restoration to the suburbs. But Timothy Keller presents an alternative perspective—that Christians should strongly consider living in cities because they have inherent values (mixed-use, walkable, diverse, dense) that are more desirable than the suburbs. Perhaps you don't disagree that cities cultivate the kinds of ideals that suburbs often destroy, but does that mean that more Christians should really move there? Can Christians make a bigger impact in this world when they live in cities?

DEBATE STARTERS

Can Christians be a greater influence on culture at large by living in big cities?

Even if we only cared about "saving souls," shouldn't the sheer quantity of people that live in urban centers compel us to live there?

How much of your decision about where to live is driven by factors that seem to be out of your control (job, family, etc.)?

How much of your decision about where to live is driven by what's convenient?

Where do you believe you could personally make the biggest difference?

*Even if you don't agree with the side you are representing, consider and offer the best arguments for your position. Be respectful.

YES

If Christians want to influence culture and make a bigger difference in our society, they should move to big cities.

THOUGHTS

NO

The suburbs are also a good place to live and are equally important for making a difference in our world.

THOUGHTS

THE RISE OF CHRISTIANITY

REFLECT

Read the following section and journal your thoughts on pages 92-93.

Sociologist Rodney Stark is one of the definitive experts on the growth of early Christianity. In his book, *Cities of God: The Real Story of How Christianity Became an Urban Movement and Conquered Rome*, he writes this:

> Within twenty years of the crucifixion, Christianity was transformed from a faith based in rural Galilee, to an urban movement reaching far beyond Palestine. In the beginning it was borne by nameless itinerant preachers and by rank-and-file Christians who shared their faith with relatives and friends. Soon they were joined by "professional" missionaries such as Paul and his associates. Thus, while Jesus's ministry was limited primarily to the rural areas and outskirts of towns, the Jesus movement quickly spread to the Greco-Roman cities, especially to those in the eastern, Hellenic end of the empire.
>
> All ambitious missionary movements are, or soon become, urban. If the goal is to "make disciples of all nations," missionaries need to go where there are many potential converts, which is precisely what Paul did. His missionary journeys took him to major cities such as Antioch, Corinth, and Athens, with only occasional visits to smaller communities

such as Iconium and Laodicea. No mention is made of him preaching in the countryside.

Paul was not a special case: it was several centuries before the early church made serious efforts to convert the rural peasantry—although many were converted by friends and kinfolk returning from urban sojourns. (HarperOne, 2007, p. 25)

REFLECTION STARTERS
Spend a few minutes journaling your thoughts to the three questions below. Then, share your reflections with the group.

What can we learn from the centrality of cities in the early growth of Christianity?

In this group gathering, you've been encouraged to consider the benefits of life and ministry in the city. How do you respond to this personally?

Does this compel you to consider living in an urban context?
If not, how does it challenge you to view your current context differently?

JOURNAL

JOURNAL

group gathering four

THE GOAL IS RESTORATION

CONCLUDE

It's never easy living in close proximity to other people. But people are important to God. And that's why cities are so important to God. When we bring restoration to the cities in which we live, we bring God's restoration to the people he loves.

Who are the people in your neighborhood or city whom you most want to see experience God's restoration in their lives?

CULTURE SHAPING PROJECT

PREPARE FOR NEXT GATHERING

Your primary assignment is to undertake your culture-shaping project before your next gathering. Be intentional about setting aside time to prepare for and execute your project so that you can discuss it when you next meet. Project options follow on pages 96-97.

CULTURE SHAPING PROJECT

IDEAS FOR GROUP PROJECT

Your group has been discussing how where you live impacts your faith. Now you have an opportunity to take what you are learning and do something together. Be sure to plan this group project early and undertake it before your final group gathering. Following are three options you might consider.

Option One: Supporting Local Businesses

Local businesses typically struggle in the face of franchises and big-box retailers. As a group, make a vow to only support local businesses for a two-week period. Whether it's a supermarket, restaurant, retailer, or the hardware store, don't shop anywhere that isn't locally owned and managed. Also, during this experiment, spend some time talking to at least one of these local business owners about how the community can better support its businesses. And consider how you can help.

Option Two: Police Car Ride-along
Your local police probably know more about the needs of your community than anyone because they see everything that happens. Most cities allow citizens to do a "ride-along," where they can ride with on-duty police officers during their shifts. Your whole group won't be able to do this together, but you could break into smaller groups of two or three. Consider doing a ride-along shift starting at midnight and going until sunrise. Much more goes on at night than you realize. Contact the police department to see if this is an option. If not, ask the police chief to meet with your group instead and talk about his or her perspective on the city.

Option Three: Meeting with the Mayor
Call your mayor's office and introduce your group as part of a faith community that wants to learn more about your city. As a group, see if your mayor or a city council member would be willing to meet for lunch or dinner. Ask questions about the needs of the city and what he or she would like to see changed. Ask how churches and groups like yours can be catalysts for the prosperity of the city. What resources do you have that could be a benefit to the city? Be sure to thank the mayor and local government for what they do (much of it goes unnoticed).

When you look at a city, it's like reading the hopes, aspirations, and pride of everyone who built it.

HUGH NEWELL JACOBSEN

What is the city, but the people? True, the people are the city.

WILLIAM SHAKESPEARE

SALT AND LIGHT

GROUP GATHERING FIVE

EVALUATING THE PROJECT

DISCUSS

Over the past several weeks, you've been exposed to some new ideas. Your group has discussed and debated how these concepts might change the way you think about faith and culture. And you've worked on a group project together to begin considering how these ideas might change the way you live your lives. Spend some time evaluating what you learned during your group project.

DISCUSSION STARTERS

How difficult was it to undertake your group project?

Did you find any part of it uncomfortable or not helpful? Why?

What's the most important thing you learned during your group project?

What long-term needs did you discover in your community?

What are some ways that you, your family, or your Society Room group could specifically address these needs?

THOUGHTS

where you live matters   101

REFLECT

JESUS IS STILL THE FOCUS

Journal your thoughts to the following questions, then share with the group.

During his famous Sermon on the Mount, Jesus said this to his disciples:

You are the salt of the earth. But if the salt loses its saltiness, how can it be made salty again? It is no longer good for anything, except to be thrown out and trampled underfoot. You are the light of the world. A city on a hill cannot be hidden. Neither do people light a lamp and put it under a bowl. Instead they put it on its stand, and it gives light to everyone in the house. In the same way, let your light shine before others, that they may see your good deeds and glorify your Father in heaven.

– Matthew 5:13-16

It's often assumed that, in this passage, Jesus is encouraging individual Christians to be good examples to others around them. While that's certainly important, Jesus is primarily addressing Christians as a group; a community of faith. In the original Greek, "you," is plural. That is, Jesus is not saying that Christians should be grains of salt or individual lights in the world (though they should be). Rather, the emphasis is on a group of people collectively being the salt, the light, for the sake of the world.

REFLECTION STARTERS

Spend a few minutes journaling your thoughts to these questions, then share with the group.

What is your church currently doing to be a redemptive and restorative presence in your neighborhood and city? How can you support those efforts?

Are there new things that your group or church should start doing for the sake of your city? What are the barriers? What are the opportunities?

JOURNAL

104 group gathering five

JOURNAL

A VISION FOR THE CITY

CONCLUDE

How do you view where you live differently as a result of this O Society Room study?

What will change about your lifestyle in the future?

What will you start doing?

What will you stop doing?

Spend the last fifteen minutes of your meeting praying as a group for your neighborhoods and city. If you've never prayed in a group, don't let this intimidate you. Your prayers need not be elaborate or articulate. Simply talk to God. Ask him to give you the strength and courage to act upon what you have learned and the patience to not grow weary in doing good. Read this passage aloud as a group before praying.

But you are a chosen people, a royal priesthood, a holy nation, God's special possession, that you may declare the praises of him who called you out of darkness into his wonderful light. Once you were not a people, but now you are the people of God; once you had not received mercy, but now you have received mercy.

Dear friends, I urge you, as foreigners and exiles, to abstain from sinful desires, which war against your soul. Live such good lives among the pagans that, though they accuse you of doing wrong, they may see your good deeds and glorify God on the day he visits us.

– 1 Peter 2:9–13

Where you live matters.

Share Your Thoughts

With the Author: Your comments will be forwarded to the author when you send them to zauthor@zondervan.com.

With Zondervan: Submit your review of this book by writing to zreview@zondervan.com.

Free Online Resources at
www.zondervan.com

Zondervan AuthorTracker: Be notified whenever your favorite authors publish new books, go on tour, or post an update about what's happening in their lives at www.zondervan.com/authortracker.

Daily Bible Verses and Devotions: Enrich your life with daily Bible verses or devotions that help you start every morning focused on God. Visit www.zondervan.com/newsletters.

Free Email Publications: Sign up for newsletters on Christian living, academic resources, church ministry, fiction, children's resources, and more. Visit www.zondervan.com/newsletters.

Zondervan Bible Search: Find and compare Bible passages in a variety of translations at www.zondervanbiblesearch.com.

Other Benefits: Register yourself to receive online benefits like coupons and special offers, or to participate in research.

ZONDERVAN®

ZONDERVAN.com/
AUTHORTRACKER